JUN 1 6 2016

CHEER CAREERS

BY CARLA MOONEY

CONTENT CONSULTANT

Pauline Zernott
Spirit Director and Coach
Louisiana State University

ABDOPUBLISHING.COM

Published by Abdo Publishing, a division of ABDO, PO Box 398166, Minneapolis, Minnesota 55439. Copyright © 2016 by Abdo Consulting Group, Inc. International copyrights reserved in all countries. No part of this book may be reproduced in any form without written permission from the publisher. SportsZone™ is a trademark and logo of Abdo Publishing.

Printed in the United States of America, North Mankato, Minnesota
082015
012016

Cover Photo: Damian Strohmeyer/AP Images
Interior Photos: John Bazemore/AP Images, 4–5; Joseph Sohm/Shutterstock Images, 6; Zach Bolinger/Icon Sportswire, 7; Aaron M. Sprecher/AP Images, 8–9; David Drapkin/ AP Images, 10; Michele Eve Sandberg/Icon Sportswire, 11 (top); James D. Smith/AP Images, 11 (bottom); Eliza Gutierrez/The Palm Beach P/ZumaPress/Newscom, 12–13; St. Petersburg Times/ZumaPress/Newscom, 14; Paul Spinelli/AP Images, 16–17; Michele Eve Sandberg/ZumaPress/Icon Sportswire, 18; Jay Bailey/Chattanooga Times Free Press/AP Images, 19; Michele Eve/Splash News/Newscom, 20; Dina Arévalo/ Valley Morning Star/AP Images, 22–23; Corey Perrine/Naples Daily News/AP Images, 24–25; Elise Amendola/AP Images, 26; Alex Brandon/AP Images, 28; Icon Sportswire/ AP Images, 29

Editor: Mirella Miller
Series Designer: Maggie Villaume

Library of Congress Control Number: 2015945768

Cataloging-in-Publication Data
Mooney, Carla.
 Cheer careers / Carla Mooney.
  p. cm. -- (Cheerleading)
 ISBN 978-1-62403-981-2 (lib. bdg.)
 Includes bibliographical references and index.
 1. Cheerleading--Juvenile literature. I. Title.
 791.6/4--dc23

                                                                        2015945768

CONTENTS

ONE
CHEER AS A CAREER

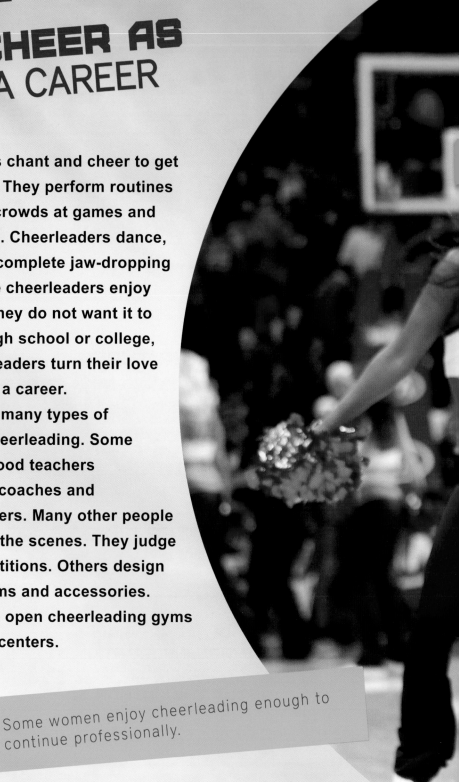

Cheerleaders chant and cheer to get fans excited. They perform routines to entertain crowds at games and competitions. Cheerleaders dance, tumble, and complete jaw-dropping stunts. Some cheerleaders enjoy it so much, they do not want it to end. After high school or college, these cheerleaders turn their love of cheer into a career.

There are many types of careers in cheerleading. Some people are good teachers and work as coaches and choreographers. Many other people work behind the scenes. They judge cheer competitions. Others design cheer uniforms and accessories. Some people open cheerleading gyms and training centers.

Some women enjoy cheerleading enough to continue professionally.

Smiling and having fun while performing encourages the crowd to have fun too.

No matter what career they choose, cheerleaders learn many skills that will help them in future cheer careers. Cheerleaders learn to work together as a team. They learn how to encourage others. They become experts at managing busy schedules and organizing events.

Sporting events are just one of the places where a professional cheerleader performs.

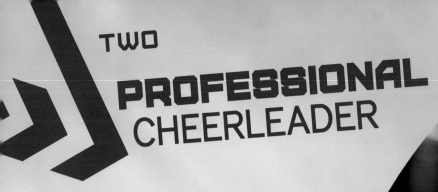

TWO
PROFESSIONAL
CHEERLEADER

Professional cheerleaders take the field on game day. They cheer, tumble, and dance. Many professional cheerleaders cheer for teams in the National Football League (NFL) and the National Basketball Association (NBA). Other professional cheerleaders cheer for teams in Canada and other countries.

Cheerleaders lead the crowd in energizing cheers. They also perform jazz and hip-hop dance routines. The NFL's Dallas Cowboys cheerleaders are one of the world's most famous professional cheerleading squads. They were the first squad to perform dance choreography in 1972.

The Dallas Cowboys cheerleaders are one of the most recognizable NFL cheer teams.

CHEERLEADING DUTIES

Professional cheerleaders spend a lot of time getting ready for game day performances. The cheerleaders arrive early before each game to stretch and warm up their muscles. Then they dance and cheer for several hours. They model for team calendars. They also perform at events. Most professional cheerleaders do not earn a lot of money. They often have another job in addition to cheerleading.

Professional cheerleading teams practice several hours every week. They might practice up to 20 hours per week during the season.

After a game, cheerleaders often stay to meet fans and sign autographs.

Cheerleaders also attend special events throughout the year.

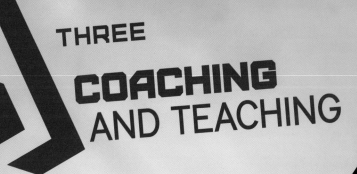

THREE

COACHING
AND TEACHING

Cheerleading coaches are leaders and teachers for cheerleaders of all ages. They encourage their cheerleaders to be the best they can be. Cheer coaches work for high schools and colleges. They also coach professional squads. Other cheer coaches work for gyms. They coach all-star squads or teach cheer classes. Some coaches work at summer camps for cheerleaders.

Cheer coaches organize and run tryouts for the squad. They judge each cheerleader and decide which ones make the squad. At practice cheer coaches teach cheerleading skills. They show the squad how to perform each move.

Coaches encourage the squad to work together as a team.

Cheerleaders need to stay in good shape to perform safely. Coaches create fitness programs to help them. These programs help increase strength. They also build and improve flexibility. Good coaches help cheerleaders become better athletes and performers.

CHOREOGRAPHER

Choreographers make cheerleading routines exciting and fun. They know how to combine dance moves, tumbling, and cheers to make a crowd-pleasing routine. They choose exciting music that energizes the crowd.

Choreographers work closely with cheerleaders to highlight their skills. They combine formations and stunts to impress the audience and judges. If a squad is performing at a competition, the choreographer makes sure the routine includes all required moves. Good choreography can help a squad win a competition.

Many cheerleading choreographers are former cheerleaders or coaches.

FOUR

BEHIND THE SCENES

Cheerleaders perform in custom uniforms. They wear special shoes and boots. They wear accessories in their hair. There are several companies that create cheer uniforms and accessories. Working for one of these companies is a great career for cheerleaders. They know what is comfortable to wear. They understand what styles and fabrics cheerleaders want to wear. There are many jobs within these companies. Designers create new and unique cheer uniforms and accessories. Salespeople work with customers to find the perfect cheer uniforms.

Uniforms must be fun, comfortable, and easy to move around in.

Many competition judges used to be former cheerleaders themselves.

Judges are watching for cheer teams to be in sync and have near-perfect routines.

COMPETITION JUDGES

Competition judges are another important part of cheerleading. Many cheerleading squads perform at competitions. They go up against other squads in front of large crowds. Judges watch all the performances. They give each squad a score. Points are awarded for each skill the squad performs. Judges give points for spirit, jump height, stunts and tumbling, precision, music, and overall performance.

Safety judges also watch each performance. They make sure the squads follow the competition's rules and are performing safely. Safety judges can take away points if a squad breaks a rule.

CHEER ADMINISTRATION

Other people work behind the scenes to make sure everything runs smoothly for a cheerleading squad or a gym. They might work on marketing programs or finding new cheerleaders. Other people work on scheduling, billing, registration, and other paperwork for the squad. Even though they are not performing in the field, all these jobs help a cheerleading squad run smoothly.

RECRUITING FOR THE DALLAS COWBOYS

Shelly Roper-McCaslin is the lead recruiter for the Dallas Cowboys cheerleaders. She has worked as a cheerleader, choreographer, and recruiter. To recruit new women, she speaks to dance studio owners and university dance team directors around the country. Before tryouts she talks to each cheerleader to get to know them. She tries to learn if they will be a good fit for the squad.

Some people work to bring new faces to professional teams' tryouts each year.

FIVE

CHEER
BUSINESSES

Some people turn their passion for cheerleading into a business. Cheer gym owners are in charge of their own gyms. They lease or buy a gym large enough for cheer, tumbling, and dance classes as well as squad practice. Then they design cheer programs for kids and adults. They set schedules for practice and camps. Gym owners select the gym's equipment. They hire cheer instructors and gymnastics coaches. Many owners are also cheerleading coaches.

Gym owners teach new moves to their students and fix any mistakes.

NO SMOKING

23

Owners are responsible for advertising their gyms. They might place ads in local newspapers or magazines. They may also pass out flyers at schools, churches, and other places to let people know about the gym.

CHEER CHANNEL

With a little creativity, cheer enthusiasts can create all types of cheer businesses. Cindy Villarreal is a former cheerleader who is the chief executive officer of Cheer Channel. This is a cheerleading news and entertainment network. The Cheer Channel has created hit Internet shows such as the *Secret Diary of an American Cheerleader* and *Cheer Mashup*. The Cheer Channel website has a lot of content for teens and tweens. It has cheer and dance news, fashion news, cheerleader profiles, and live and taped competitions.

In order to have a busy and successful gym, owners must advertise and work hard.

Kelly Bennion, second from right, has to keep up with her schoolwork and a full cheerleading schedule.

KELLY BENNION

Kelly Bennion is a professional cheerleader for the NFL's New England Patriots. She is also a full-time student pursuing a degree in neuroscience. Bennion has been dancing since the age of seven, learning jazz, tap, and ballet. Before cheering for the Patriots, she cheered for her high school squad. She also danced

on the Harvard Crimson Dance Team while in graduate school. Bennion is a member of Science Cheerleader.

SCIENCE CHEERLEADER

Darlene Cavalier is a former cheerleader who started her own cheer business. She created Science Cheerleader. This organization encourages young women interested in cheerleading to think about careers in science, technology, engineering, and math. Science Cheerleader members include nearly 250 former and current professional cheerleaders. These women have careers in science or are currently studying science. Science Cheerleader works with several groups, including the National Science Foundation. Together they created an award-winning video series called *Science of NFL Football*.

With a lot of hard work and determination, you can turn cheerleading into a career.

CHEER SEATTLE

CHEER Seattle is a nonprofit adult cheerleading squad. They do not perform for a sports team. Instead the squad performs to raise awareness and money for charities. CHEER Seattle has performed at events such as the American Lung Association's Fight for Air Climb in Seattle, Washington.

With some creativity and dedication, it is possible to turn cheer into a career. Some people choose to stay in the field and perform as professionals. Others decide they want to give back and teach the next generation of cheerleaders. Some people stay involved in cheer behind the scenes, working with squads or dreaming up new cheer businesses. The love of cheer can become a lasting career!

Cheerleaders work hard to pump up the crowd at sporting events.

GLOSSARY

AUTOGRAPH
The signature of someone famous.

CHOREOGRAPHER
Someone who organizes dance moves and creates routines.

COMPETITION
The process of trying to win something that someone else is also trying to win.

FLEXIBILITY
The ability to stretch and move easily without injury.

FORMATION
An arrangement or pattern that cheerleaders stand in during a routine.

NEUROSCIENCE
The study of nerves and how they affect behavior.

ROUTINE
A series of movements that are repeated for a performance.

SQUAD
A small group doing the same activity, often a physical activity.

STUNT
An exciting and sometimes dangerous move or jump during a cheer routine.

TUMBLING
Gymnastic skills such as somersaults and handsprings.

FOR MORE
INFORMATION

BOOKS

Farina, Christine, and Courtney A. Clark. *The Complete Guide to Cheerleading: All the Tips, Tricks, and Inspiration*. Minneapolis: MVP, 2011.

Webb, Margaret. *Pump It Up Cheerleading*. New York: Crabtree, 2012.

Webber, Rebecca. *Varsity's Ultimate Guide to Cheerleading*. New York: Little, 2014.

WEBSITES

To learn more about Cheerleading, visit **booklinks.abdopublishing.com**. These links are routinely monitored and updated to provide the most current information available.

INDEX

ABOUT THE AUTHOR

Carla Mooney is the author of several books for young readers. She loves reading and learning about different careers. A graduate of the University of Pennsylvania, she lives in Pittsburgh, Pennsylvania, with her husband and three children.